Moray Eel

by Jen Green

Consultants:

John E. McCosker, PhD
Chair of Aquatic Biology, California Academy of Sciences

Maureen Flannery, MS
Ornithology and Mammalogy Collection Manager, California Academy of Sciences

Wallace J. Nichols, PhD
Research Associate, California Academy of Sciences

BEARPORT
PUBLISHING

New York, New York

Credits

Cover, © Fred Bavendam/Minden Pictures/FLPA; 3, © Hugh Russell/Shutterstock; 4, © Dan Exton/Shutterstock; 5, © Imagebroker/FLPA; 7, © Stephen Frink/RGB Ventures LLC dba Superstock/Alamy; 8–9, © Ethan Daniels/Shutterstock; 10, © Dreamstime; 11, © Dray van Beeck/Shutterstock; 12TL, © Colin Marshall/FLPA; 12TR, © Dan Exton/Shutterstock; 12BL, © Pavel Borowka/Shutterstock; 12BR, © Shutterstock; 13, © NHPA/Photoshot; 14–15, © iStockphoto/Thinkstock; 16–17, © Reinhard Dirscherl/FLPA; 18, © Barb Makohin/Liquid Life Photography; 19, © Dreamstime; 20–21, © Rienhard Dirscherl/FLPA; 22TL, © Norbert Probst/Imagebroker/FLPA; 22TR, © Kim Briers/Shutterstock; 22CL, © Dreamstime; 22CR, © Liquid Productions LLC/Shutterstock; 22BL, © Dreamstime; 23TL, © Dan Exton/Shutterstock: 23TC, © Barb Makohin/Liquid Life Photography; 23TR, © Brandon D. Cole/Corbis; 23BL, © Stephan Kerkhofs/Shutterstock; 23BC, © NHPA/Photoshot; 23BR, © Arie Wolde/Shutterstock.

Publisher: Kenn Goin
Editorial Director: Adam Siegel
Creative Director: Spencer Brinker
Photo Researcher: Brown Bear Books Ltd

Library of Congress Cataloging-in-Publication Data

Green, Jen.
  Moray eel / by Jen Green.
    p. cm. — (The deep end: animal life underwater)
  Includes bibliographical references and index.
  ISBN 978-1-61772-921-8 (library binding) — ISBN 1-61772-921-3 (library binding)
  1. Morays—Juvenile literature. I. Title.
  QL638.M875G74 2014
  597.43—dc23
                    2013010804

For more information, write to Bearport Publishing Company, Inc., 45 West 21st Street, Suite 3B, New York, New York 10010. Printed in the United States of America.

10 9 8 7 6 5 4 3 2 1

Contents

A Hidden Danger

Some brightly colored fish swim through a coral reef.

Nearby, a moray eel pokes its head out of a little cave.

It watches the fish swim by.

Suddenly, the eel darts out.

In a flash, the moray grabs its **prey** with its sharp, pointy teeth.

moray eel

4

Coral reefs are rock-like structures. They are made up of the skeletons of sea animals called coral polyps. Many kinds of sea creatures find homes, food, and hiding places in reefs.

moray eel

coral reef

What kind of animal do you think a moray eel is?

5

Moray eels look a lot like snakes, but they are really fish.

Like all fish, they live and breathe underwater using body parts called gills.

However, morays are different from most other fish.

Their bodies are very long and thin, and they swim by wiggling through the water.

Also, their skin is smooth and not covered by **scales**.

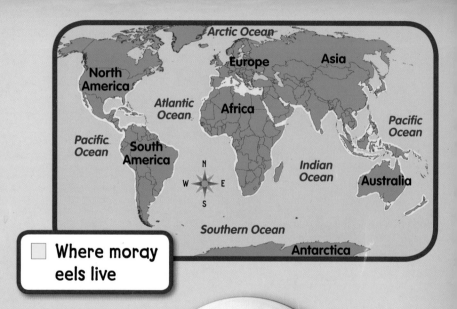

☐ Where moray eels live

There are about 200 kinds of moray eels. They live in many parts of the world, mostly in shallow, warm ocean waters.

6

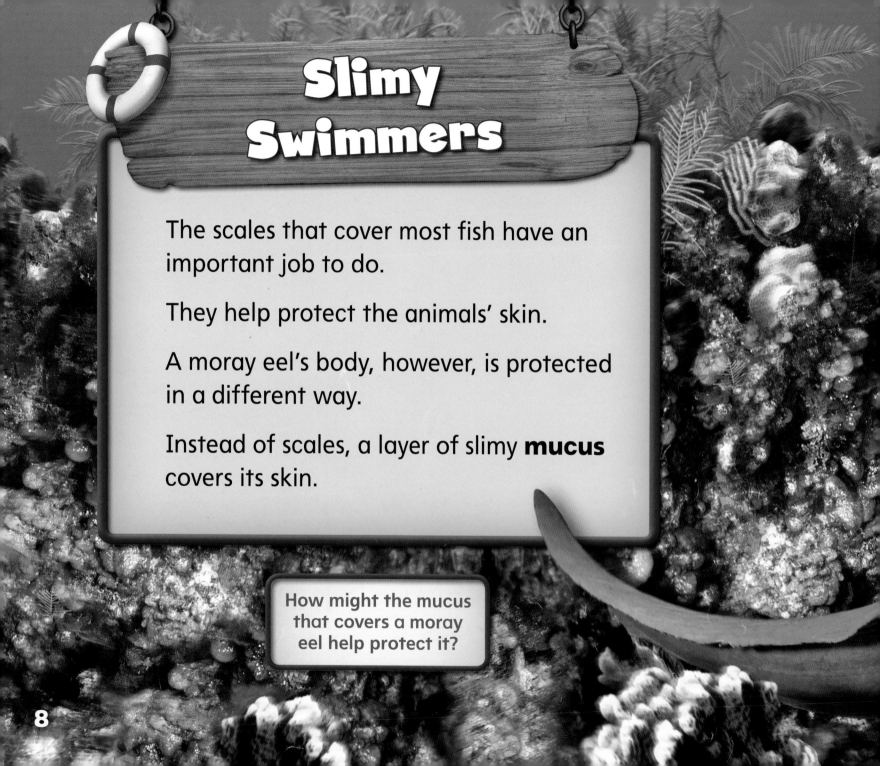

Slimy Swimmers

The scales that cover most fish have an important job to do.

They help protect the animals' skin.

A moray eel's body, however, is protected in a different way.

Instead of scales, a layer of slimy **mucus** covers its skin.

How might the mucus that covers a moray eel help protect it?

Moray eels can be large or small. The biggest grow to 13 feet (4 m) in length—as long as two tall men lying head to toe. The smallest are less than five inches (13 cm) long.

green moray eel

slimy skin

Staying Out of Sight

A moray eel can squeeze its long, thin body into narrow cracks between rocks.

Its slimy covering keeps it from getting cut as it moves.

Most of the time, however, the eel doesn't swim around.

Instead, it watches and waits in its hiding place, called a **lair**.

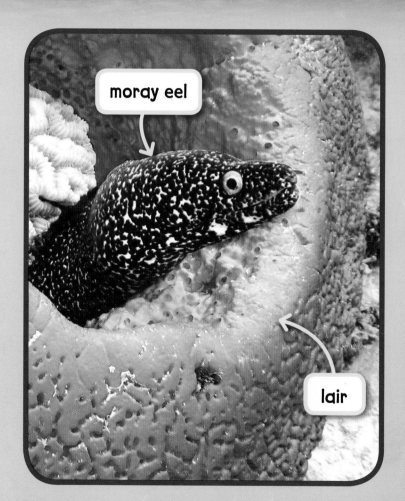

moray eel

lair

Eel Meals

Moray eels hunt and eat other animals.

Fish and squid are their favorite foods.

The eels grab these creatures as they swim by their lairs.

Their curved, needle-sharp teeth keep a tight grip on the slippery prey.

When is the safest time for moray eels to leave their lairs?

Moray Eel Food

sea snake

squid

fish

sea urchin

12

moray eel

octopus

Moray eels also eat octopuses and hard-shelled animals, such as crabs.

Day and Night

During the day, a moray eel mostly lurks in its lair.

If enough fish or squid swim by, the eel can find food without leaving its cave.

At night, however, a hungry eel might leave its lair to go hunting.

In the dark, animals are less likely to spot an eel on the move.

At night, moray eels cannot see well. They mostly track down food using their sharp sense of smell.

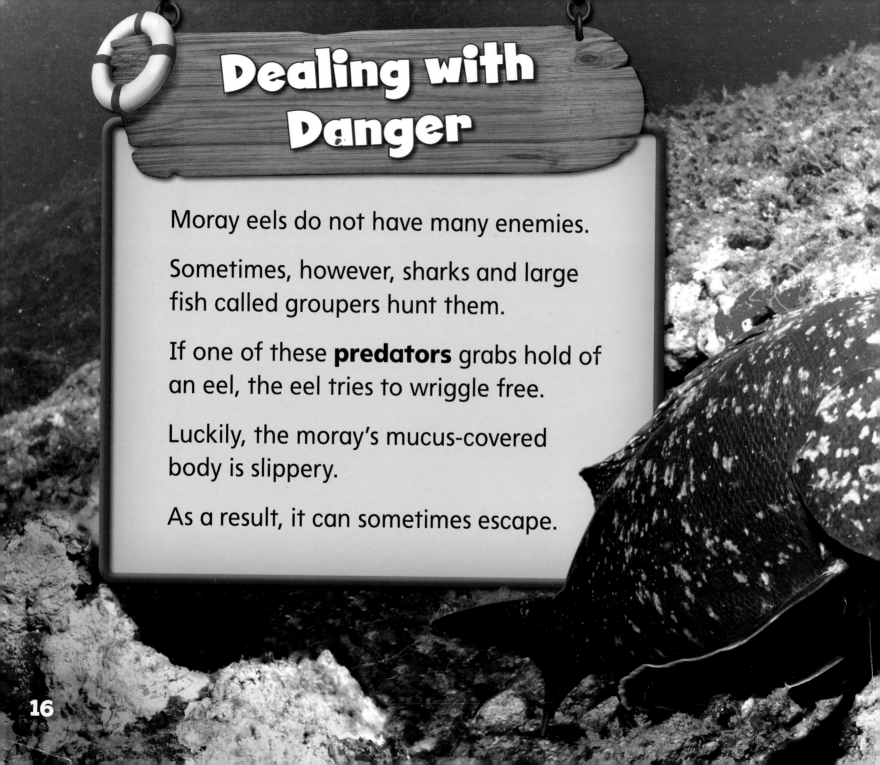

Dealing with Danger

Moray eels do not have many enemies.

Sometimes, however, sharks and large fish called groupers hunt them.

If one of these **predators** grabs hold of an eel, the eel tries to wriggle free.

Luckily, the moray's mucus-covered body is slippery.

As a result, it can sometimes escape.

Baby Morays

Like most fish, moray eels hatch from eggs.

A mother eel lays thousands of eggs in the ocean.

After about a month, the eggs hatch.

The babies that come out are called **larvae**.

They look like long, narrow leaves.

eel larva

At first, eel larvae have see-through bodies and are almost invisible.

young moray eel

How might laying
so many eggs help
moray eels survive?

Growing Up

After hatching, moray eel larvae float to the surface of the ocean.

Other fish eat most of them, but some survive.

The babies grow longer and more eel-shaped.

After about a year, they swim to the bottom of the ocean.

There, they hide in rocks and reefs.

They are still small, but they begin to live like grown-up eels—waiting and watching.

Be an Eel Scientist!

Different kinds of moray eels have different colors and patterns on their bodies.

Imagine you are a scientist who studies eels.

Look at the colors and patterns of the eels on this page.

Now match the photographs to the descriptions at the bottom of this page to find out the name of each kind of eel.

(The answers are on page 24.)

A

B

C

D

E

- Blue and yellow = ribbon moray eel

- Green = green moray eel

- Purple with white rings = zebra moray eel

- Orange, purple, and white = dragon moray eel

- Yellowish white = giant moray eel

Science Words

lair (LAIR) a hole or cave that is used as a hiding and resting place

larvae (LAR-vee) baby eels after they have hatched from eggs

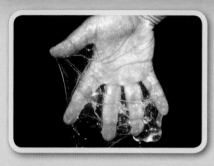

mucus (MYOO-kuhss) a slimy liquid made by an animal

predators (PRED-uh-turz) animals that hunt and kill other animals for food

prey (PRAY) an animal that is hunted by another animal for food

scales (SKAYLZ) small, thin plate-like parts that cover the bodies of fish

Index

Read More

Goldish, Meish. *Moray Eel: Dangerous Teeth (Afraid of the Water).* New York: Bearport (2010).

Rand, Casey. *Giant Morays and Other Extraordinary Eels (Creatures of the Deep).* Chicago: Raintree (2012).

Zobel, Derek. *Eels (Oceans Alive).* Minneapolis, MN: Bellwether Media (2008).

Learn More Online

To learn more about moray eels, visit **www.bearportpublishing.com/TheDeepEnd**

Answers

- A is a giant moray eel • B is a zebra moray eel
- C is a dragon moray eel • D is a green moray eel • E is a ribbon moray eel

About the Author

Jen Green has been interested in natural history since she was a child. She has written dozens of children's books, on subjects as varied as raccoons, gophers, and termites. She loves walking in her native Sussex, England.